GOLF'S LITTLE
INSTRUCTION BOOK

GOLF'S LITTLE INSTRUCTION BOOK

Hundreds of Wise Suggestions

Arthur Witebsky

A BIRCH LANE PRESS BOOK
Published by Carol Publishing Group

A Birch Lane Press Book
Published by Carol Publishing Group
Citadel Press is a registered trademark of Carol
    Communications, Inc.
Editorial, sales and distribution, rights and permissions
    inquiries should be addressed to Carol Publishing
    Group, 120 Enterprise Avenue, Secaucus, N.J. 07094
In Canada: Canadian Manda Group, One Atlantic
    Avenue, Suite 105, Toronto, Ontario M6K 3E7

Carol Publishing Books are available at special discounts
for bulk purchases, sales promotion, fund-raising, or
educational purposes. Special editions can be created to
specifications. For details, contact: Special Sales
Department, Carol Publishing Group, 120 Enterprise
Avenue, Secaucus, NJ 07094.

Manufactured in the United States of America
10 9 8 7 6 5 4 3 2 1

Library of Congress Cataloging-in-Publication Data
Witebsky, Arthur.
    Golf's little instruction book : hundreds of wise
suggestions / Arthur Witebsky.
        p.   cm.
    "A Birch Lane Press book."
    ISBN 1-55972-355-6 (hardcover)
    1. Golf.   I. Title.
GV965.W74   1996
796.352—dc20   95-50090
                                                    CIP

ACKNOWLEDGMENTS

I HAVE BEEN BLESSED with two parents whom I love and respect more than anyone could ever know. Everything that I am or will ever become I owe to them. Thank you for making my life so enjoyable and wonderful. My brother David, the most honest and caring person I will ever know, taught me more about myself than I sometimes cared to know. Sumner, thank you for welcoming me into your family and home. If you can put up with me, you can put up with anything. Shaun, you are what makes the world a wonderful place, and you truly are my inspiration. Kim, there would be no book without your help and motivation. Allison, I will always love you. Thanks go to my friends Wayne, John Paul, and Nicole and so many others for their friendship and support. To all the wonderful people I've golfed with, thank you for teaching me about life and golf.

INTRODUCTION

THIS BOOK CAME not out of the desire to teach people how to play the game of golf, but rather to teach people how to respect one another on the course and give helpful hints on what to do before and after playing golf. I hope these little tips will truly help both beginners and advanced golfers, as well as non-golfers. At the very least, I hope that it will drive home the point that both on and off the golf course we must all learn to respect one another and live in peace and harmony.

GOLF'S LITTLE
INSTRUCTION BOOK

- Have fun.

- Yell, "Fore!"

- Hit new balls when playing a round.

- Hit clean balls.

- Keep your head still and behind the ball.

- Ask other golfers how they are playing.

- Wear golf shoes.

- Walk on pavement every now and then. Spikes sound good, and the sound makes you feel like you really play golf.

- Take your jewelry off before playing.

- Compliment other golfers after a good shot.

- Be the first one to introduce yourself to your playing partners.

- Help others look for their ball.

- Don't step in the line of someone else's putt.

- Fix ball marks.

- Replace divots.

- Play quickly—try not to slow other groups.

- Let smaller, quicker groups play through.

- Wear a hat.

- Wear a collared shirt.

- Put shoe trees in your golf shoes after each use.

Golf is twenty percent mechanics and technique. The other eighty percent is philosophy, humor, tragedy, romance, melodrama, companionship, camaraderie, cussedness, and conversation.

GRANTLAND RICE

- Be positive and optimistic—think you are going to play well.

- Don't make golf your only exercise.

- Remember that uphill putts are usually easier than downhill putts.

- Don't swing at the ball; swing through it.

- Be thankful that you have the means and ability to play the game—Lord knows, millions don't.

- Stare at the ball, not your club, during the backswing.

- Get behind the ball and/or the hole to read the break of putting greens.

- Don't use Mickey Mouse golf club covers.

- Don't look up to see your putt—looking up will not make the putt go in the hole. Concentrate on the stroke and stare at the ball.

- Wear two pairs of socks in cold weather.

- Put your wallet and your keys in your golf bag before playing.

- Stay balanced during and after your swing.

- Learn from your bad shots; study them.

- Learn a few trick shots.

- A good golf course should be measured by the friendliness of the staff.

- Keep your eyes over the ball while putting.

- Don't expect to be a pro right away. Golf takes years and years of practice.

- Ask permission from your playing partners to hole out short putts.

- Attach a tag with your name on it to your golf bag.

- Put your name, address, and phone number on your putter and wedges.

- Write down and keep track of your golfing goals.

- Wait until the group ahead of you is definitely out of range before playing your shot.

- If you see lightning, get inside immediately. Trees are not inside.

- Keep your clubs in your car. You never know when or where a golf course or range will appear.

- Think of your swing as a pendulum—the ball lies on a small arc made by that pendulum.

- Keep your back foot planted.

- Don't look for a lost ball for more than three minutes.

- Buy a ball retriever. It will pay for itself quickly.

You can't go into a shop and buy a good game of golf.

SAM SNEAD

- Your body shouldn't move on putts—only your arms. Long putts are the exception.

- Practice using every club in your bag.

- On the practice green or any green, use one ball and pretend par is always two.

- Pack an extra pair of socks for those not-so-beautiful days.

- Have a golf hero. Find out about the player, not the golfer.

- Get your tee times early. As golf gets more popular, courses are getting more crowded.

- Use the practice green before every round of golf.

- Flip a tee to see who hits first. Whomever the tee points to hits first.

- Avoid gimmicks. Nothing beats real golf and real practice.

- Your clubhead and body need to be aimed at the target.

- Decide exactly how you are going to play each and every shot before you take it. Indecision will add strokes to your score.

- Don't litter on the course.

- Don't drive your car while wearing your golf shoes.

- Don't wear your golf spikes in the house. This will keep you out of big trouble.

- On practice swings, try to hit something. Never swing at nothing.

It's nothing new or original to say that golf is played one stroke at a time. But it took me many years to realize it.

BOBBY JONES

- Keep sunscreen in your bag.

- Remember your starter or professional on holidays.

- Attach your wood covers to your bag.

- Think you are going to make every putt.

- Compliment aspects of your playing partner's swing, no matter how ugly it might be.

- Perform the same routine before every shot.

- Take a set of clubs to the driving range before you decide to purchase them.

- Test different clubs—especially woods and wedges.

- Play country club courses.

- Play public courses.

- Keep score for beginners.

- Never cheat.

- Never play at a club that discriminates.

- Keep aspirin in your bag.

- Carry Band-Aids in your bag.

- Carry insect repellent in your bag.

- If you ever use a caddy, give him or her a big tip.

- Remember to stretch before a round, especially your back muscles.

- Ladies hit first.

- See the movie *Caddyshack*. Again.

- Accept advice graciously, even when you know you will never follow it.

- After a bad shot, forget about it. Don't let it affect your next shot and ruin the rest of your day.

- Never quit a round, regardless of how bad you're playing.

- When holding two clubs on the green, hand one to someone to hold or place it on top of your golf bag—you'll avoid losing your clubs.

- Resist the temptation to comment on someone's swing. It's OK to make a helpful statement or compliment, but don't suggest that they try something.

- Keep your golf bag clean and organized.

- Don't let a bad hole get you down. There are seventeen other holes on the course on which you can improve.

- Avoid foods high in sugar like candy bars and sodas. Eat natural sugars such as fruits and juices.

- Buy your partners lunch or drinks after a good round.

- Celebrate personal records.

- If you don't like your partner, stay focused on your game.

- Learn how to lose graciously. It's easy: just act like a winner.

- Keep track of your scores and personal goals in a journal.

- Save and collect scorecards.

- Learn specific course and club rules before playing.

- Never try to crush the ball. Swing smooth and easy.

The man who can putt is a match for anyone.

WILLIE PARK JR.

- Never throw clubs or balls.

- Keep your emotions under control. Smile! It's a great game.

- Avoid placing your bag on the fringe around the greens.

- Try to keep driving carts off the fairways.

- Play easy golf courses occasionally to boost your confidence.

- Walk the course if you can; it's just that much more exercise.

- Follow through like a pro—at least you'll look good.

- Visit Myrtle Beach, South Carolina. Play a lot and eat well.

- If you can afford it, go to England and Scotland. Play the legendary courses such as St. Andrews, Turnberry, and Royal Lytham.

- Visit the 19th hole and talk about your game.

- Learn from golf tournaments on TV.

- Visualize your shots as you want them to be.

- Maintain self-confidence, no matter how badly or with whom you are playing.

- If you are right-handed, keep your left arm straight.

  If you are left-handed, keep your right arm straight.

- Carry coins in your pocket.

- Wear a glove.

- Golf with an elder.

- Golf with a youngster.

- Don't shave strokes—every stroke counts.

- Putt all of your putts. Nothing is a "gimme."

- Rake bunkers.

After taking the stance, it is too late to worry. The only thing to do is hit the ball.

BOBBY JONES

- Keep a set of extra tees in your pocket.

- The beauty of a swing does not matter—look at Arnold Palmer.

- Stop and enjoy the natural beauty of a golf course.

- Support the USGA.

- Always keep score.

- Take your spouse and/or family out to dinner after a weekend of golf to remind yourself that there are other things more important than golf.

- A quick fix is OK for a round. Just make sure to find a long-term solution.

- Practice your putting—remember, it's half the game.

- Don't take shortcuts on your swing. Learn to do it right.

- Turn golf carts off or stop as others are hitting nearby.

- Subscribe to golf magazines.

- Challenge yourself by playing different courses.

- Study the scorecard to learn about each hole before you play it.

- Keep your shadow out of others' view as they are hitting.

- Hold the flag, not just the pole when tending the pin.

- The person whose ball is closest to the hole should tend the flag for others in the group.

- Don't stand behind the hole as others are putting.

- Don't drop the flag; lay it down.

- Small wagers never hurt.

- Don't talk or whisper while others are hitting.

- Don't curse. Keep the game clean and gentlemanly.

- Never take your shirt off.

- Get your spouse involved in the game.

- Attend a professional golf tournament.

- Play in charity tournaments, regardless of your ability.

- Keep an umbrella in your bag.

- Clean your clubs yourself.

- When you hit the green, take a long walk with your putter.

- Get to know your starter.

- Eat and drink something between the 9th and 10th holes.

*T*here are a couple of
"could'ves" in every round.

ALLEN GEIBERGER

- At the driving range, don't just hit balls, aim for targets.

- Determine the average distance that you hit each club at the driving range.

- Pass the baton. Help get young kids involved in the game.

- Use a light grip.

- Never drink excessively on the course.

- You don't need to be big and strong to play golf—look at Corey Pavin.

- Set a goal for yourself every time you play a round of golf.

- Practice pitching in a park.

- Read the *Rules of Golf*.

- Play by the *Rules of Golf*.

- Take a mulligan every now and again.

- Keep a plastic water bottle in your golf bag.

- People on the fringe hit first, regardless of distance to the hole.

- The person farthest from the hole hits first.

- Play with honors—the person with the lowest score on the previous hole hits first.

- Attach a towel to your bag.

- Study videotapes of your swing.

- Stay out of view as someone is hitting.

- Before you get frustrated by the slow group in front of you, remember how you first played the game.

- Always mark and clean the ball before putting.

- Clean the path of the ball before putting.

- Keep some deodorant in your bag.

- Learn about the many traditions of golf.

*T*he pat on the back, the arm around the shoulder, the praise for what was done right and the sympathetic nod for what wasn't are as much a part of golf as life itself.

GERALD FORD

- Volunteer your time for a golf tournament.

- A round isn't over until your ball hits the bottom of the 18th hole.

- Get a good travel bag for your clubs. Don't rely on a top bag cover alone.

- Keep extra pencils in your bag.

- Wear golf ties.

- Play miniature golf with your family and friends.

- Play quietly.

- Let your son or daughter beat you every now and then.

- Read golf books.

- Buy a commemorative ball from each course you play and save it!

- Plan a golf weekend just for the guys.

- Help your partners rake their bunkers.

- Don't carry a big tour bag.

- Play with the best clubs you can afford.

- Get a comfortable shoulder strap for your bag.

- Get an official handicap.

- Have a handshake and a warm thank-you ready for your playing partners at the end of each round.

- If you're paired with other play- ers, be absolutely certain that you remember their names.

- Don't be afraid to change your swing.

- If you're comfortable with your swing and not scoring well, a change might be necessary.

- If you smoke, ask your playing partners if it's OK to smoke. Ninety-nine percent of the time they'll say no problem. It's simply polite to ask first.

- Buy waterproof golf shoes or waterproof your current ones.

*T*he friends you make on the golf course are the friends you make for life.

JESSICA ANDERSON VALENTINE

- Get your golf professional's opinion regarding a new golf club purchase. Not all golf clubs are right for you and your swing.

- Go to see a Senior PGA tour event. These are the gentlemen that helped make golf the great game it is today.

- Never brag about your game.

- If you can't make a tee time, call ahead to cancel so others can play in your slot.

- Nothing beats an afternoon nap after an early-morning round of golf!

- Never bring beepers, pagers, or cellular phones to the golf course. Help keep golf a game.

- Call an old friend that you
  haven't seen in a while and play
  a round of golf. It's the best way
  to rekindle a friendship.

- Try to play at least once a week.
  It's good for you!

- Look at your swing in a mirror.
  You'll see both the good and the
  bad.

- Stay informed about the PGA tournaments; it'll give you that much more to talk about with your playing partners.

- It's better to be known as a great person to play with than as a great golfer.

- Smile a lot; people will think you're playing well.

- Don't be too proud to take lessons.

- Support the LPGA tour.

- Play the most difficult courses in town. The other courses will seem that much easier.

- Keep your game dress, demeanor, and play simple. After all, golf is a simple game.

- Walk off greens quickly after finishing. Remember, the groups behind you are anxious to hit.

- Keep an extra ball in your pocket.

- When watching professional golfers be sure to analyze elements of their swing, i.e., stance, ball position, leg movements, grip, etc...

I've found that to be truly successful in the world of golf one must first come to accept himself as a human being who has the inner capabilities to improve and become a better person.

GARY PLAYER

- Pack a light jacket or sweater in your bag.

- Visit the Golf Hall of Fame in Pinehurst, North Carolina.

- Clean and dry your clubs after each round. You don't want dirty or rusty clubs to start you next round.

- Wipe your clubs after each shot.

- Support programs which give underprivileged kids an opportunity to play and learn about golf.

- Play golf with someone who is physically disadvantaged. That person will make you see the world in a different light.

- Don't leave wet golf shoes in the trunk of your car. Phew! No one ever does it twice.

- Encourage and support young kids on the golf course. Never get frustrated or angry with them. They will remember how they were treated. Let them learn to enjoy the beauty and grace of the game.

- Learn golf terminology. There's so much of it, it's almost like learning a foreign language.

- Never wear black socks with shorts.

- Dry your hands before hitting.

- On hot, sunny days stand in the shade when possible.

- Place a mark on all of your golf balls.

- Use two hands when replacing the flag—the lip of the cup will thank you.

- When asked about how other golfers play, always reply, "Very well." Nothing more need be said.

- Practice what you're bad at, not what you're good at!

- Don't throw away old clubs.

- Buy golf prints and pictures.

- If possible, go to the U. S. Open at least once in your lifetime.

- If you see geese on the course, watch your step. You don't want to step in anything.

- If you can't shower, at least wash your hands and face after a round.

If there's one thing golf demands above all else, it's honesty.

JACK NICKLAUS

- Play your ball as it lies. Winter rules don't always apply.

- Bring a sand wedge to the beach—it's one big sand trap.

- Send golf-themed Christmas cards.

- Have at least one picture of yourself golfing.

- Wear light-colored clothing to stay cool.

- Wear cotton.

- Wear loose clothing.

- Show up at least fifteen minutes before your scheduled tee time.

- Personal hygiene means a lot on the golf course.

- Don't pound the ball washer; lift and lower the handle slowly.

- Help your playing partners determine yardage to the flag.

- Use the Porta-Johns.

- Practice hitting from difficult
  and different lies.

- Take your business cards with
  you to the golf course. You
  never know who you might meet.

- If you have the opportunity, play
  in a pro-am. You'll never forget
  the experience.

The way you are on the golf course is usually the way you are in life.

TAMMIE GREEN

- Have a favorite golf club.

- Give golf gifts to friends who golf.

- Support the Junior USGA.

- Clean out your golf cart when finished.

- After you make a birdie, leave a dollar bill in the hole.

- Keep your swing in shape in winter—try playing indoor simulated golf.

- Always help a lady.

- Play golf video games.

- Buy golf calendars.

- Buy golf coffee table books.

- Don't play golf when you're not in the mood—it's meant to be enjoyed and savored.

- If you need glasses, wear contacts at the course.

- Eat lightly before playing a round—save your appetite for later.

- Always watch your playing partners hit—it's courteous and you can help them locate their ball.

- First learn how to hit the ball well, then worry about scoring well.

- Don't be short on your shots.

- Starters always receive a great deal of grief. Give him or her a compliment and a thank-you instead.

- Just because you golf, it doesn't mean that you have to wear *ugly* plaids.

- Be competitive and still have fun. Learn from Fuzzy Zoeller.

- If you do make small wagers, settle them before leaving the golf course.

- Learn to laugh at your bad shots.

The spirit, the will to win, and the will to excel are the things that endure, these qualities are so much more important than events that occur.

VINCE LOMBARDI

- Every couple of months, drive a couple of hours out of town to play a new or different golf course.

- Don't make excuses after bad shots. Everyone is playing the same course as you!

- Return lost golf clubs to the clubhouse after your round.

- Carry breath mints or gum in your golf bag. They'll help get rid of that early-morning coffee breath.

- Learn about the hundred greatest golf courses in America.

- Who says you can't play golf in the snow and rain?

- Refuse to lose.

- Let your kids drive your golf cart for you.

- If playing partners are not familiar with golf etiquette, don't hesitate to teach them. It will help them and anyone else they play with.

- Join the USGEA—the United States Golf Etiquette Association. Call 301-221-8433.

- Every now and then play 36 holes a day.

- Use the restrooms *before* you walk onto the golf course.

- Leave your sunglasses at home.

- After a bad round, don't even think about quitting golf. Concentrate on how well you are going to play the next round.

- Read Harvey Penick's *Penick's Little Red Book*.

- Compliment other golfers on their clothes or clubs. It'll make them feel that much better.

- Golf only after the yard work is done.

- Donate an old set of clubs to an orphanage.

- Bring a putter and golf balls to the office.

- Hit golf balls on your lunch break.

Good things come to those who wait.

HARRISON DILLARD

- Once a year, on a truly spectacular day, call in sick and play 18 holes. Live a little.

- Know the difference between a Surlyn and Balata ball, and how each affects your game.

- When planning a vacation, reserve your tee times at least one week before leaving.

- Play in the rain at least once—
  you'll appreciate the sunny days
  much more.

- Try playing with oversized clubs.

- Send away for *Myrtle Beach Golf
  Holiday* magazine—P.O. Box
  1323, Myrtle Beach, South
  Carolina 29578-1323. It's free!

- Never wear cutoff jeans.

- Keep a handkerchief or tissues in your bag.

- Give the service workers at your club or course a bonus or gift at Christmas time.

- Offer a little encouragement to a friend who is playing poorly.

- Watch the starters board so you and your group don't get skipped or passed.

- Learn to take compliments well. A thank-you is always appreciated.

- Never criticize another player. If you can't say anything nice, don't say anything at all.

- Every now and then take some
  pictures at the golf course—
  you'll appreciate the memories.

- Find out if your golf club or
  course is environmentally safe.
  If not, suggest that the club
  become certified by the Audubon
  Cooperative Sanctuary Program.

- Change out of your spikes before
  using the restroom.

- Try to get the Golf Channel. Golf coverage and lessons twenty-four hours a day!

- Keep in mind that practice putting greens are sometimes a different speed than the greens on the course.

- Buy stock in a golf-related business.

Without heroes, we are all plain people and don't know how far we can go.

BERNARD MALAMUD

- Remove grass and debris from your spikes before entering the clubhouse.

- Never spit.

- Don't chew tobacco on the course.

- When changing in the locker room, don't take up all the space on the bench.

- Wear at least a towel in the locker room.

- If you get a chance to play in Europe, stop in Spain to play Valderrama.

  Play in Hawaii.

- Don't even think about playing golf on your honeymoon.

- Buy "kiddie clubs" for your children for Christmas, Hanukkah or birthdays.

- Have a miniature golf birthday party for your child and his friends.

- Golf balls make a great stocking stuffer.

- Don't play with an orange ball in the fall.

- Never bring glass bottles on the golf course—use cans.

- Dress well when attending a golf tournament.

- Follow the designated paths on the course. Don't create your own.

If you have things in order and realize golf is not the most important thing in the world, you will probably be okay without it.

BOB ESTES

- Always wear a belt.

- It is a golfer's dream to die on the golf course.

- Rent instructional golf videos.

- When taking a long car trip, buy or rent a golf audio book.

- Wear green during Masters week.

- Don't just record your total score, but record the number of putts taken on each hole.

- At least once a year play a round with the entire family.

As long as a person doesn't admit he's defeated, he is not defeated—he's just a little behind and isn't through fighting.

DARRELL ROYAL

- Send a thank-you note after playing with business associates.

- Let your spouse beat you every now and then.

- On really cold days, pack a small thermos. It will help to warm your insides and your hands.

- At least once a year, take and teach someone who has never played before.

- While on a trip, record the names and addresses of players you are paired with. You never know when you might be in their neck of the woods and have the time to play.

- Have your company picnic at a local golf course.

*R*emember, it is not about winning or losing, but rather how you play the game.

ANONYMOUS

- Don't cancel rounds with playing partners; otherwise they will be less likely to invite you the next time.

- Give tickets to a golf tournament to someone who can't afford them.

- Take care to store your clubs properly in the winter.

- Get to know new acquaintances by inviting them to play golf.

- Encourage your child to join the golf team.

- Play during non-peak hours; you'll save a couple of bucks at most public courses.

I'm not going to get it close,
I'm going to make it.

Tom Watson

- For the consideration of others, always accompany small children to the golf course.

- Invite your in-laws to play golf. It's a good place to make peace.

- If possible, buy a retirement home on a golf course.

- Carry lip balm.

- Don't use golf as an excuse to skip going to church or synagogue.

- Send a golf care package to golfing friends who live far away.

- Never store your clubs in a closet. Keep them within sight.

- Never place your bag on the green.

- For your lunch break, go eat lunch at a golf course and enjoy the atmosphere.

- Try the Top-Flite Magna golf ball—it could help your game.

- Replace worn or missing spikes.

- The best is not always the most expensive.

- Expect to pay for quality merchandise.

- Get personalized golf license plates.

- For superb golf information about schools and publications, call the National Golf Foundation.

*B*e a dreamer. If you don't know how to dream, you're dead.

JIM VALVANO

- If you have the means, play golf at Pebble Beach.

- If you can't play Pebble Beach, play a simulated version.

- When driving a car or cart on a golf course, drive slowly.

- Offer to carry a lady's golf bag to and from the clubhouse.

- Always look your partners in the eye when introducing yourself.

- Learn about the various games you can play to create extra excitement, such as Nassau, Wolf, and Hawk.

- At a golf tournament, go watch the players practice on the putting green and the driving range.

- After a great round, have a playing partner attest the scorecard—it'll validate your score and prove to be a great memento.

- Keep your eyes on the ball; don't assume you know where it's going. Watch it until it comes to rest.

- Take your hat off while eating in the clubhouse.

- Send friends and family post-
  cards from each of the golf
  courses you play—especially
  when on vacation.

- Consider a Disneyworld vacation
  to satisfy both the kids and your
  golfing urges.

- Loosen the flagstick before
  someone putts. You'll avoid
  damaging the lip of the hole
  when pulling the flag out.

- Follow the career of Tiger Woods—he's a great person, and is going to be a great golfer.

- In the winter, try to find a driving range with heated golf tees.

- Hang golf pictures in your office.

- Don't get defensive when someone says golf is boring. Chalk it up to inexperience.

- If your putts haven't been falling, make a change.

- Shave before a round. Don't look scruffy.

- Practice by placing your ball in poor lies, not good ones.

- Your mental abilities can conquer a lack of physical abilities.

- Remember, it's the pressure shots that count the most.

- You need your vision to play golf. Have it checked yearly.

- Never be afraid of a golf shot—conquer it!